Recipes by Julie Daurel

Grilling

Photographs by David Japy
Styling by Florence des Grottes

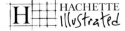
HACHETTE
illustrated

contents

Fruit and vegetables

grilling – Spanish style

Plancha cuisine

Plancha cuisine is Spanish in origin. Its first appearance dates from the nineteenth century, during the *romerías*, which were the feasts that occurred during the pilgrimages. During these celebrations, huge steel hot plates were set on top of glowing embers and used as cooking surfaces. This ingenious method allowed them to cook a large number of chickens and vegetables side by side. The plancha was born. Eventually gas burners replaced the hot coals as a heating method.

In the 1970s, the method of cooking spread rapidly in the Basque region of Spain, where it was used for large gatherings at sporting and culinary events. It quickly caught on and soon bars were using this method to cook tapas for the cocktail hour, including grilled slices of chorizo sausage, tiny squid and boletus mushrooms.

A simple utensil

A plancha is usually made from enameled steel, measuring 20 x 20 inches square or reaching as much as 20 x 40 inches. A hole pierced in one of the corners allows cooking juices to drain into a small ceramic pot. The cooking surface is supported by a metal frame. Heat comes from one, two or three burners linked to a gas cylinder.

It can be placed on a heatproof surface, made from heat-resistant brick or concrete. For more flexibility, it can also be installed on a trolley.

For safety reasons, a plancha should only be used outdoors, or in a very well ventilated area, at least 3 feet from all flammable items.

Another form of plancha is a cast iron griddle that has a ridged surface to sear and grill meat, fish, and vegetables. The flat reverse side can be used for pancakes and crêpes.

Easy to maintain

As soon as the plancha is cool enough to handle, wash it with a non-abrasive sponge, washing up liquid, and water. Abrasive sponges will scratch the surface and should not be used.

If the cooking surface is very dirty, plug the drainage hole and soak the surface with a combination of water and vinegar. Let stand, overnight if necessary, then use a wooden spatula to scrape up the cooked on bits.

If cooking several batches of food that are not necessarily compatible (fish and meat, for example), drizzle the surface with vinegar or sea salt. Let the salt dissolve then wipe clean to remove any odors. The plancha will then be ready for cooking the next batch of food.

Healthy eating

A plancha is the ideal way to prepare a wide range of fresh ingredients: vegetables, meat, fish, and seafood. Its ability to maintain a constant high temperature means that delicate ingredients can be cooked to perfection – tender and full of flavor on the inside, crisp on the outside.

The shape of a plancha means that several ingredients can be cooked at the same time by simply arranging them on different sides of the cooking surface, say, vegetables on one side and fish or meat on the other.

A distinct advantage of plancha cusine is that the ingredients all cook evenly without risk of flare ups.

Easy to prepare

Before cooking, preheat the plancha for 5 minutes on high heat.

Ladle a little oil or other fat onto the cooking surface.

The temperature depends on whether you want to cook quickly over high heat or slowly on low heat. It is possible to have several different temperatures on the surface at the same time by controlling the level of flame for each burner. In this way, you can cook meat or fish on one side, while you keep the sauce and vegetable accompaniment warm on the other.

Wooden tongs and spatulas are the best utensils to use with a plancha. Never pierce the surface of ingredients as they cook. Firstly, they will lose all the flavorsome juices and also, it could damage the enameled surface.

Sauces and marinades

Plancha cooking is straightforward and easy. Using marinades and other dressings help to give a bit of originality to your dishes.

Choose from traditional marinades or lemon juice, soy sauce, or spices. A marinade will tenderize and enhance the flavor of meat, fish, and vegetables before they are grilled.

A classic vinaigrette dressing is one of the best sauces for this type of cuisine. Its outdoor nature goes well with ingredients such as fresh herbs, balsamic vinegar, and lemon juice.

Be adventurous and experiment with different taste combinations. Surprise your friends – the sky's the limit!

Grilled baby squid

Serves 6

3 lb whole baby squid

3 tablespoons olive oil

2 tablespoons lemon juice

4 garlic cloves

1 bunch flat leaf parsley

salt and freshly ground black pepper

Clean the squid, pulling out the innards and removing the outer membrane. Rinse well and pat dry with a paper towel.

Cut into pieces and toss with the oil.

Slice the garlic and mix into the lemon juice. Chop the parsley and set aside.

Heat a steel hotplate, cast iron griddle, or barbecue.

Add the squid and cook until they begin to brown, about 10 minutes, turning with a wooden spoon.

Add the lemon juice and garlic and cook for a further 2-3 minutes.

Season with salt and pepper and sprinkle with the parsley.

Serve with a crisp green salad.

Tuna and bacon kabobs

Serves 6

2 lb fresh tuna

10 thin slices unsmoked bacon

12 cherry tomatoes

olive oil

shreds of lemon peel, pared off with a zester

For the marinade:

2 tablespoons lemon juice

1 red onion, finely chopped

½ teaspoon cayenne pepper (see note)

6 bay leaves, roughly torn

2 teaspoons salt

wooden skewers, presoaked to prevent burning

Combine all the marinade ingredients in a bowl.

Cut the tuna into 1-inch cubes. Toss in the marinade and let stand overnight.

The following day, when ready to serve, roll up the tuna in strips of bacon that have been cut to the same width. Thread onto the wooden skewers, alternating with cherry tomatoes and pieces of bay leaf.

Heat a plancha, cast iron griddle, or barbecue.

Mix a little olive oil and the lemon zest in a small bowl. Brush onto the tuna kabobs.

Cook the kabobs on the plancha or griddle, for 5–10 minutes each side.

Note: If you can find piment d'Espelette, which is a speciality hot red pepper from the Basque region of France, all the better, but cayenne pepper is an acceptable substitute.

Salmon with herbs and sea salt

Serves 6

6 salmon fillets

2 tablespoons olive oil

1 shallot

3 oz unsalted butter, softened

3 tablespoons each chopped fresh flat leaf parsley, dill, and chives

sea salt

Choose boneless salmon fillets. However, keep the skin on.

Heat a plancha, cast iron griddle, or barbecue.

Rinse the salmon and pat dry with a paper towel. Brush the skin side with oil.

Peel and chop the shallot finely. Combine with the butter and herbs, and mix well. Set aside.

Cook the salmon fillets, skin side down, on the hot plancha or griddle (which should be hot, but not smoking). To make sure the skin is crispy, cook for 20 minutes over a steady, moderate heat. The salmon should still be slightly underdone.

Transfer to warmed plates. Sprinkle each fillet with a little sea salt and a knob of herb butter. Serve immediately.

Porgy Spanish-style

Serves 6

2 garlic cloves, peeled

1 small dried red chile

2 sea bream (porgy), gutted and scaled

1 cup olive oil, plus extra 2 tablespoons

4 tablespoons sherry vinegar

sea salt and freshly ground black pepper

Slice the garlic and chile and set aside.

Dry the fish with paper towels and brush each fish with the 2 tablespoons olive oil.

Heat a plancha, cast iron griddle, or barbecue.

In a pan, heat the remaining oil and gently fry the sliced chile and the garlic slices until they are golden. Stir in the vinegar and cover straightaway to avoid splattering. Keep warm.

Cook the fish on the plancha or griddle, 10–15 minutes on each side.

Transfer the cooked fish to serving plates. Slice in half lengthwise and remove the bones. Season with salt and pepper and pour over the garlic oil. Serve immediately.

Angler fish medallions with bell pepper sauce

Serves 6

3 lb (in 2 pieces) angler fish tail

1–2 garlic cloves, peeled and sliced

12 bacon strips

2 tablespoons olive oil

For the bell pepper sauce:

3 tablespoons olive oil

2 large onions, sliced

2 cans red bell peppers

1 cup sour cream, or thick yogurt

½ teaspoon saffron

½ teaspoon curry powder

salt and freshly ground black pepper

Cut the angler fish fillets away from the bone and remove the grey membrane.

Make several incisions in the fillets and insert slivers of garlic, according to taste. Wrap the 2 fillets together in the bacon strips, like a roast, and secure with kitchen string. Refrigerate until needed.

For the sauce: heat the oil in a pan, add the onions and cook until soft. Drain the bell peppers, slice, and add to the onions. Simmer gently for 30 minutes, stirring frequently.

Stir in the sour cream, saffron, and curry powder. Season with salt and pepper. Purée in a blender until smooth. Keep warm in a dish which is immersed in hot water, half way up its sides, in a roasting pan (bain marie).

Heat a plancha, cast iron griddle, or barbecue.

Cut the wrapped fish into thick slices, about the width of a bacon strip. Brush liberally with oil, and season lightly with salt and pepper.

Cook the slices on the hot plancha or griddle, about 5 minutes each side. Serve with the bell pepper sauce.

Scallops with fresh cilantro

Serves 6

3 red bell peppers

6 sun-dried tomatoes

24 raw fresh scallops

5 tablespoons olive oil

1 tablespoon lemon juice

1 teaspoon honey

cayenne pepper (see note on page 8)

3 sprigs fresh cilantro

salt and freshly ground black pepper

Preheat the oven to 425°F

Put the bell peppers in the oven and roast for 30 minutes. Remove, let cool, then peel, discard the seeds, and cut the flesh into small dice.

Thinly slice the sun-dried tomatoes and mix with the bell peppers. Season lightly with salt and pepper.

Rinse the scallops under cold running water and pat dry with a paper towel.

In a shallow dish, combine 4 tablespoons of the olive oil, the lemon juice, honey, 2 pinches of salt, and the cayenne pepper. Mix well, then add the scallops. Marinate for 15 minutes, turning once.

Heat a plancha, cast iron griddle, or barbecue.

Heat the remaining tablespoon of olive oil on the plancha or griddle. Add the bell pepper mixture and cook, stirring for 2–3 minutes. Add the scallops and cook for 50 seconds on each side.

Sprinkle with the cilantro and serve.

Sardines with pastis

Serves 6

36 sardines, each about 4-5 inches long

1 lemon

4 garlic cloves, crushed

3 tablespoons pastis (anise-flavored liqueur)

5 tablespoons olive oil

3 tablespoons chopped flat leaf parsley

salt and freshly ground black pepper

lemon wedges

Arrange the sardines in a large shallow dish. Pare a few strips of rind from the lemon and squeeze the juice. Add the lemon juice and rind, garlic, pastis, oil, and half of the parsley to the fish. Toss well to mix, then allow to marinate in the refrigerator for 30 minutes.

Heat a plancha, cast iron griddle, or barbecue.

Remove from the fish from the marinade. Cook on the hot plancha or griddle, 3–4 minutes on each side.

Season the sardines with salt and pepper and serve immediately with lemon wedges.

This dish is delicious accompanied by a salad made from lambs' lettuce, thinly sliced fennel, and oranges.

Grilled mussels with piment d'Espelette

Serves 6

4 lb fresh mussels, cleaned (see note)

For the chili sauce:

7 ripe tomatoes, cored, peeled, seeded, and chopped

1 tablespoon ground piment d'Espelette (see note on page 8)

$2/3$ cup water

5 garlic cloves, finely chopped

1 small onion, finely chopped

salt

In a pan, combine the tomatoes, piment d'Espelette, and water. Bring to a boil and cook over high heat until the tomatoes are cooked, about 15 minutes. Stir in the garlic and a good pinch of salt. Stir in the onions and check seasoning.

Heat a plancha, cast iron griddle, or barbecue.

Cook the mussels over medium heat for 10 minutes. Discard any mussels that have not opened.

Serve in the shell, with the sauce on the side for dunking.

This dish makes an ideal appetizer. To serve as a main course, double the quantities and serve with rice or pasta.

Note: It is essential to clean the mussels thoroughly. Place in a basin of cold water and discard any that float to the surface. Scrape off the beards and any barnacles with a sharp knife under running water. Discard any that are broken or open and refuse to shut when tapped sharply with the knife. Leave the cleaned mussels in a basin of clean, cold water until ready to cook to loosen any remaining grains of sand.

Mixed shellfish and Spanish sausage

Serves 6

2 lb cockles

2 lb mussels

1 lb clams

2 medium to large tomatoes

1 celery heart

2 longanisses (anise flavoured Spanish sausage)

1 oz salted butter

1 tablespoon olive oil

1 dried red chile

1 garlic clove

2 tablespoons chopped parsley, to garnish

salt and freshly ground black pepper

Soak the cockles in some cold water and then wash in several changes of fresh water to remove the sand. Rinse and clean the other shellfish (see note on page 20).

Peel, seed, core, and chop the tomatoes. Cut the celery into thin slices.

Heat a plancha, cast iron griddle, or barbecue, to low.

Purée the sausage and garlic in a food processor.

Melt the butter and oil on the plancha or griddle, add the celery and cook for 2 minutes. Add the tomatoes and crumble over the chile with your fingers (make sure you wash your hands after handling the chile, and take care to not wipe your eyes). Season with salt and pepper, and cook for 3 minutes.

Put the shellfish on the plancha or griddle and raise the heat. Cook, stirring, until the shells open. Discard any that do not open. Stir in the garlic–sausage mixture and cook for a few minutes. Sprinkle with parsley and serve hot.

Variation: The longanisses sausage can be replaced with chorizo or any other spicy sausage.

Peppered shrimp

Serves 6

36 large shrimp

8 tablespoons peanut oil

2 tablespoons black peppercorns

2 tablespoons soy sauce

4 stalks fresh lemongrass, finely chopped

sea salt

Heat a plancha, cast iron griddle, or barbecue.

Heat the oil on the plancha or griddle and cook the shrimp for 4 minutes on each side.

Scatter with the peppercorns and lemongrass and season with the soy sauce and sea salt.

Serve very hot.

Marinated lamb chops

Serves 6

12 lamb chops

For the marinade:

4 tablespoons olive oil

8 tablespoons red wine

2 shallots or 1 onion, finely chopped

2 garlic cloves, finely chopped

1 tablespoon chopped mixed fresh herbs (parsley, thyme, rosemary)

salt and freshly ground black pepper

In a shallow dish, combine all the marinade ingredients and mix well. Add the chops, toss to coat and marinate for 2 hours at room temperature.

Heat a plancha, cast iron griddle, or barbecue.

Remove the chops from the marinade and cook over high heat, about 5 minutes on each side.

Veal kidney brochettes

Serves 6

3 veal kidneys

8 oz pancetta in a piece, or bacon

3 heads Belgian endive

3 radicchio

a few sprigs of thyme and parsley, to garnish

For the vinaigrette:

5 tablespoons olive oil

2 tablespoons sherry vinegar

1 small fresh red chile, sliced

1 garlic clove, crushed

salt and freshly ground black pepper

wooden skewers, presoaked to prevent burning

Cut the kidneys into cubes and remove the white parts. Steep the kidney cubes for 1 hour in water to which a little vinegar has been added. Drain and pat dry with a paper towel.

Cut the pancetta, or bacon, into pieces about the same size as the kidney cubes.

Thread the kidney pieces on the skewers, alternating with pieces of pancetta. Allow 2 skewers for each person.

Steam the Belgian endive and radicchio for 10 minutes; they should retain some crunch.

For the vinaigrette: whisk together the oil and vinegar with 1 tablespoon of water. Add the slices of chile and the crushed garlic, and season with salt and pepper.

Heat a plancha, cast iron griddle, or barbecue.

Cook the brochettes over high heat, about 10 minutes on each side. About 5 minutes before the end of cooking, put Belgian endives and radicchio on the plancha or griddle.

Serve the kidneys and vegetables, drizzled with the vinaigrette and sprinkled with the herbs.

T-Bone steaks with marrow

Serves 6

2 marrow bones

6 tablespoons red wine

3 tablespoons finely chopped shallots

2 T-bone steaks, about 1³/₄ lb each, or 6 smaller steaks, depending on the appetite of your guests

5 oz salted butter

1 tablespoon lemon juice

2 tablespoons chopped fresh parsley

sea salt and freshly ground black pepper

Scoop out the marrow from the bones and poach in boiling water for 10 minutes.

Heat a plancha, cast iron griddle, or barbecue.

Drain the marrow and chop coarsely. Keep warm to one side of the grill.

In a small pan, combine the wine and shallots and cook until reduced. Set aside.

Heat 2 tablespoons sea salt on the plancha or griddle, then add the steaks and cook for 5 minutes on each side (or for longer or shorter, depending on how rare or well-cooked the diners prefer). Turn with tongs, not a fork, to avoid piercing the meat and letting all the juices escape.

Let rest on one side of the plancha.

Reheat the shallot mixture. Remove from the heat and whisk in the butter, continuing to whisk until well blended. Stir in the lemon juice and parsley. Season with salt and pepper and transfer to a warm sauceboat. Keep warm to one side of the plancha.

Cut the beef into slices and discard the bones, or serve as whole steaks, depending upon the size. Serve hot, drizzled with the sauce and sprinkled with marrow pieces.

Grilled chicken with fresh vegetables

Serves 6

1 large chicken, about
4 lb, or 2 small chickens,
cut into pieces

3 bell peppers (1 green,
1 red, 1 yellow), seeded
and sliced

6 small zucchini, cut in
half lengthwise

1 bundle asparagus

large handful black olives,
to garnish

For the marinade:

10 garlic cloves, crushed

1¼ cups lemon juice

½ cup olive oil

3 tablespoons fresh
rosemary leaves

salt and freshly ground
black pepper

Combine all the marinade ingredients. Season with salt and pepper. Put the chicken pieces in a shallow dish, add two-thirds of the marinade and mix well. Pour the remaining marinade over the vegetables. Marinate in the refrigerator for at least 2 hours.

Heat a plancha, cast iron griddle, or barbecue.

Cook the chicken; allow 10 minutes for the breast pieces and 20 minutes for the others. Cook the vegetables, about 5 minutes on each side, drizzling with the remaining marinade.

Make sure that the chicken is cooked through by piercing the fattest area with a sharp skewer to check that the juices are clear.

Serve the pieces of chicken with the vegetables, scattered with the olives.

Duck breasts with onion marmalade

Serves 6

3 duck breasts

salt and freshly ground black pepper

For the onion marmalade:

4 onions

1 oz salted butter

²/₃ cup grenadine syrup

²/₃ cup wine vinegar

1 tablespoon balsamic vinegar

pinch of cayenne pepper

1¼ cups golden raisins

For the onion marmalade: peel the onions and chop finely. Heat the butter in a skillet, add the onions and cook over low heat, stirring frequently, until soft. Do not allow the onions to brown. Stir in the grenadine and both vinegars. Season with salt and pepper. Add the cayenne pepper and golden raisins and stir well. Lower the heat and cook gently until the onions are melted and the liquid is almost completely evaporated, about 1½ hours.

Heat a plancha, cast iron griddle, or barbecue.

Cook the duck breasts on the plancha or griddle, starting with the skin side down, for 10 minutes. Using tongs, turn the duck and cook the other side for 10 minutes. Let stand for 5 minutes, then slice the duck thinly. Season with salt and pepper and serve with the onion marmalade.

Rabbit with bacon, herbs and tapenade

Serves 6

4 tablespoons olive oil

2 tablespoons lemon juice

3 teaspoons dried herbes de Provence, or mixed herbs

3 garlic cloves, crushed

2 small rabbits, cut in pieces

10 slices pancetta, or bacon

salt and freshly ground black pepper

3 tablespoons chopped fresh marjoram or oregano

black olive tapenade and garlic mayonnaise, for serving

Combine the oil, lemon juice, dried herbs and garlic. Season with salt and pepper. Rub this mixture all over the rabbit pieces and leave to marinate at room temperature for 1 hour.

Heat a plancha, cast iron griddle, or barbecue.

Remove the rabbit pieces from the marinade and pat dry. Reserve the marinade. Wrap each piece in pancetta or bacon and tie with kitchen string to secure.

Cook the rabbit over medium heat, 30–35 minutes, turning regularly and basting with the marinade.

Serve hot, sprinkled with the marjoram, and with black olive tapenade and garlic mayonnaise on the side.

Marinated chicken and Dublin Bay prawn brochettes

Serves 6

8 tablespoons lemon juice

3 tablespoons olive oil

3 tablespoons curry powder

5 chicken breasts

15 raw Dublin Bay prawns (or lobsterettes)

1¼ cups long grain rice

½ pineapple

1 red apple

knob of salted butter

salt and freshly ground black pepper

wooden skewers, presoaked to prevent burning

In a shallow dish, combine the lemon juice, olive oil, and 1 tablespoon of the curry powder. Season with salt and pepper and mix well.

Cut the chicken breasts into cubes. Peel the Dublin Bay prawns, leaving only the tail end. Thread alternate pieces of chicken and prawn on the skewers. Allow 2 brochettes per person.

Marinate the brochettes in the lemon juice mixture for 1 hour, turning occasionally.

Cook the rice in twice its volume of water that has been salted and seasoned with the remaining 2 tablespoons of curry powder.

Heat a plancha, cast iron griddle, or barbecue.

Slice the pineapple and cut the apple into cubes. Melt the butter on the plancha or griddle and cook the fruit over low heat, for 10 minutes. Keep warm to one side of the plancha.

Raise the heat and cook the brochettes, allowing 3–5 minutes each side.

Put the rice and fruit in a large dish and arrange the brochettes on top. Serve hot.

Lamb burgers with sheep's milk cheese

Serves 6

¾ cup milk

3 cups fresh breadcrumbs

2 lb minced lamb

1 egg plus 2 yolks

4 tablespoons olive oil

salt and freshly ground black pepper

6 bread rolls

6 slices sheep's milk cheese (Brousse, or Emmenthal, if preferred)

6 slices mild onion

6 tomato slices

6 lettuce leaves

mustard or ketchup, to serve

Combine the milk and breadcrumbs. Mix with the minced lamb. Add the 2 egg yolks and mix well. Season with salt and pepper. Divide into 6 equal portions and shape into burgers.

Put the remaining egg in a bowl and beat well. Coat the burgers in the egg.

Heat a plancha, cast iron griddle, or barbecue. Brush with the olive oil.

Cook the lamb burgers over high heat, about 5 minutes each side, until browned and crispy.

Split the bread rolls and toast lightly on the plancha or griddle. Fill with the burgers, top each with a cheese slice and garnish with the onion, tomato and lettuce. Serve with ketchup or mustard as desired.

Veal rolls with green tapenade and anchovies

Serves 6

1 veal fillet

salt and pepper

For the tapenade:

2 cups anchovy-stuffed olives, drained

1½ oz unsalted butter

2 tablespoons olive oil

pinch of cayenne pepper

2 tablespoons drained capers

24 wooden cocktail sticks

Put the veal in the freezer for 1 hour. Remove and slice thinly

For the green olive tapenade, purée the olives, butter, oil, Cayenne pepper, and capersin a food processor. Taste for seasoning and adjust as necessary. Chill in the refrigerator until needed.

Heat a plancha, cast iron griddle, or barbecue.

Grill the veal slices until golden on both sides. Set aside to cool. Shape the veal slices into small cones and fill with the tapenade. Secure the cones with cocktail sticks.

Serve with drinks or as a light appetizer, accompanied by a crispy green salad.

Eggplant rolls with goats' cheese

Serves 6

2 large eggplants

5 tablespoons olive oil

8-oz piece goats' cheese

3 tablespoons chopped fresh sage

salt and freshly ground black pepper

For the sauce:

1 cup natural yogurt

3 garlic cloves, crushed

1 tablespoon finely chopped fresh mint

12 wooden cocktail sticks, presoaked

With a sharp knife, cut each eggplant into 6 long, thin slices.

Heat a plancha, cast iron griddle, or barbecue.

Brush the eggplant slices with olive oil on both sides. Season with salt and pepper, then cook over medium heat, 3–4 minutes each side, until tender. Set aside.

For the sauce: combine the yogurt, garlic, and mint. Season with salt and pepper and place in the refrigerator until needed.

Cut the goat's cheese into 12 pieces. Sprinkle the cheese with some of the sage. Roll up the cheese pieces in the eggplant slices and secure with cocktail sticks.

Cook the eggplant and cheese rolls on the plancha or griddle for 3 minutes each side. Serve hot, with the yogurt sauce on the side, for dunking.

Basque vegetable skewers

Serves 6

1 whole head garlic

2 onions

12 shallots

2 zucchini

1 chorizo sausage

9 small, firm tomatoes

18 bay leaves

2 tablespoons olive oil

salt and freshly ground black pepper

2 sprigs fresh thyme, to garnish

18 wooden skewers, presoaked to prevent burning

Separate the garlic cloves and peel. Peel the onions and cut into wedges. Wash the zucchini and cut into thick sticks. Cut the chorizo into rounds. Rinse the tomatoes and cut into wedges. Blanch the shallots in boiling water for 2 minutes, then drain and cut into half lengthwise.

Heat a plancha, cast iron griddle, or barbecue.

Thread the vegetables on to 9 of the skewers, alternating the garlic cloves, chorizo, onions, and tomato wedges.

On the remaining 9 skewers, arrange the zucchini, shallots, and bay leaves. Season with salt and pepper and brush with olive oil. Cook for 5 minutes on each side.

Sprinkle with thyme leaves before serving.

Grilled wild mushrooms

Serves 6

2 lb boletus (fresh porcini) mushrooms, or chestnut mushrooms

2 garlic cloves

bunch of parsley

6 egg yolks

knob of butter

salt and freshly ground black pepper

Carefully wipe the mushrooms to remove all traces of dirt. Cut into slices.

Heat a plancha, cast iron griddle, or barbecue.

Crush the garlic, snip the parsley leaves with scissors and mix with the garlic. Set aside.

Melt the butter on the plancha or griddle and cook the mushrooms over high heat until browned.

Transfer to warmed plates. Place an egg yolk on the side of each plate. Season all over with the garlic mixture, salt, and pepper.

Dip the mushrooms into the egg yolk before eating.

Note: As an alternative, serve a soft-boiled egg separately for each person, as shown in the photograph.

Raw or lightly cooked eggs should be avoided by vulnerable people such as pregnant and nursing mothers, invalids, the elderly, babies, and young children.

Artichoke heart and chorizo fricassee

Serves 6

2 large red onions

2 lb small artichokes

2 tablespoons olive oil

½ spicy chorizo sausage, sliced

1 teaspoon honey

2 tablespoons chopped parsley

salt and freshly ground black pepper

Peel the onions and cut into slices.

Remove all the tough outer leaves from the artichokes to expose the tender hearts. Cut each heart into six pieces.

Heat a plancha, cast iron griddle, or barbecue.

Heat the oil on the plancha or griddle, add the onions and cook over low heat until soft. Add the sliced artichoke hearts and cook, stirring constantly, until the artichokes are tender.

About 5 minutes before the end of cooking, add the sliced chorizo and the honey. Season with salt and pepper and sprinkle over the parsley. Stir well and serve very hot.

Warm mushroom salad with tarragon

Serves 6

**8 medium mushrooms,
about 14 oz**

olive oil

**1 plate of cooked polenta,
cut into cubes**

**3 Belgian endives, sliced
thinly lengthwise**

handful of fresh arugula

handful of red leaf lettuce

3 shallots, chopped

**salt and freshly ground
black pepper**

For the marinade:

**1 tablespoon balsamic
vinegar**

**2 tablespoons chopped
tarragon**

2 tablespoons olive oil

3 tablespoons hazelnut oil

4 tablespoons pine nuts

For the marinade: combine half of the balsamic vinegar, half of the tarragon, and half the hazelnut oil. Add the olive oil.

Slice the mushrooms and put in a shallow dish. Season with salt and pepper and pour over the marinade. Let stand at room temperature for 45 minutes.

Heat a plancha, cast iron griddle, or barbecue.

Brush the plancha or griddle with olive oil. Cook the polenta cubes until browned. Drain the mushrooms and cook over medium heat, 1–2 minutes on each side.

Meanwhile, combine the endives, arugula, red leaf lettuce, and shallots. Season with the remaining balsamic vinegar and hazelnut oil.

Arrange the warm polenta cubes and mushrooms on top of the dressed leaves. Sprinkle with the pine nuts and the remaining tarragon.

Garlic-marinated bell peppers

Serves 6

2 green bell peppers

2 red bell peppers

2 yellow bell peppers

For the garlic marinade:

6 tablespoons olive oil

4 tablespoons lemon juice

4 garlic cloves, crushed

1-2 tablespoons fresh rosemary leaves

salt and freshly ground pepper

Combine all the marinade ingredients.

Cut the bell peppers into slices and discard the seeds. Rinse under cold water, then pat dry with a paper towel. Leave to marinate for 1 hour at room temperature.

Heat a plancha, cast iron griddle, or barbecue.

Remove the bell peppers from the marinade and reserve the marinade. Grill the bell peppers for 20 minutes, turning often.

Season with salt and pepper and drizzle with the marinade.

Carrot and squash fries

Serves 6

1 bunch young carrots

2 lb squash

olive oil

2 tablespoons chopped chervil

salt and freshly ground pepper

Peel the carrots and squash. Cut the vegetables into French-fries-sized batons.

Steam the carrots for 10 minutes.

Heat a plancha, cast iron griddle, or barbecue.

Brush the vegetables with olive oil and grill, turning frequently, until evenly browned all over.

Sprinkle with chervil, season with salt and pepper, and serve.

Grilled oranges with strawberries

Serves 6

6 oranges

6 tablespoons confectioners' sugar

3 tablespoons Grand Marnier liqueur

12 oz strawberries, prepared, thinly sliced, and sprinkled with sugar

Cut the peel from the oranges with a sharp knife, removing as much pith as possible. Slice the oranges into rounds.

Put the orange slices in a shallow dish and sprinkle with the sugar. Pour over the liqueur. Let stand for 15 minutes.

Heat a plancha, cast iron griddle, or barbecue.

Cook the oranges over high heat for 3–4 minutes. They should be browned with a slightly caramelized surface.

Serve immediately, with the strawberries.

Peach salad with marzipan and macaroons

Serves 6

6 peaches

4 tablespoons confection-ers' sugar

1 tablespoon vanilla sugar, or 1 tablespoon caster sugar with a 1/4 teaspoon vanilla extract

4-oz piece marzipan, crumbled

about 10 macaroons

Poach the peaches in gently simmering water for 1 minute, to soften the skin. Peel the peaches and cut each one into quarters, discarding the pits.

Heat a plancha, cast iron griddle, or barbecue.

In a pan, combine the butter and sugars over low heat until melted. Brush over the peach pieces.

Grill the peaches, about 5 minutes on each side.

Transfer the warm fruit to serving dishes. Sprinkle with crumbled pieces of marzipan and serve accompanied by the macaroons alongside.

Figs with raspberries, honey, and Greek yogurt

Serves 6

6 tablespoons honey

3 tablespoons dry white wine

18–24 firm, ripe figs

2 cups fresh raspberries

2 cups Greek yogurt

In a pan, combine the honey and wine over low heat and stir until the honey is completely melted. Set aside.

Heat a plancha, cast iron griddle, or barbecue.

Halve the figs and brush with the honey mixture. Grill over medium heat for 2–3 minutes, basting with the honey mixture.

Serve the figs hot, in bowls, with the raspberries and yogurt.

The concept for this book came from Forges Adour, plancha makers for more than two decades. Forges Adour Tel: (33) 5 59 42 42 02.

Props
Planchas: Forges Adour
Basque linens: Artiga, Jean-Vier, Moutet
Plates and cutlery: Jean-Vier, Terafeu-Terafour

Text and styling: Julie Daurel
Home Economist: Florence des Grottes
Photographs: David Japy

© Hachette Livre (Marabout) 2003
This edition published in 2004 by Hachette Illustrated UK, Octopus Publishing Group Ltd., 2–4 Heron Quays, London E14 4JP

English translation by JMS Books LLP (email: moseleystrachan@blueyonder.co.uk)
Translation © Octopus Publishing Group Ltd.

A CIP catalog for this book is available from the Library of Congress

ISBN: 1 84430 085 4

Printed by Tien Wah, Singapore